Blue Hues & Infinite Loops: A Collection of Poetry

Megan Matos

BookLeaf Publishing

India | USA | UK

Presentation by *BookLeaf Publishing*

Web: www.bookleafpub.com

E-mail: info@bookleafpub.com

ISBN: 9789360948276

First edition 2024

To the community of readers who find solace in a diverse collection of poetry that loosely fits the mold.

To my beloved wife, cherished son, supportive parents, and close-knit inner circle.

ACKNOWLEDGEMENT

I am deeply thankful for all those people in my life who believed in me, showed their support, and encouraged me to write.

I first want to thank my parents who helped foster my love for the written word from a very early age. Thank you for bolstering this passion by supplying me with copious amounts of notebooks, journals, planners, and of course gel pens (typical millennial thing to say).

To my beloved wife, Andrea, I extend appreciation for her unwavering support and encouragement in my creative pursuits. Thank you for inspiring me to confidently pursue my writing goals and reconnect with my creative spirit.

And to our son, Julian, who reminds me every day of the joy and freedom that comes with creative expression. His curiosity and imagination are a constant source of inspiration, and I'm grateful for the opportunity to witness his creative spirit blossom.

It is my everyday life that motivates me and my desire to write. I am thankful for this human experience and the ability to articulate about the very things that fuel my creativity.

PREFACE

Hello Reader!

Welcome to "Blue Hues & Infinite Loops," my debut collection of poetry inspired by my life and the natural world around me. In these pages, you'll find yourself immersed in a sea of blue hues, each line a reflection of the emotions that course through me.

Amidst the shades of blue, you'll also encounter the infinite loops of life; a gentle reminder that it's all a cycle with moments of joy, love, pain, and everything in between - repeating and evolving endlessly.

I invite you to immerse yourself in the world of "Blue Hues & Infinite Loops." I hope you find solace, joy, and a deeper understanding of the colorful hues, and limitless loops in your life within its pages.

Thank you for reading and embarking on this journey with me.

With gratitude,
Megan Matos

Echoes of the Rain: Nature's Ballet

Clouds roll in, heavy, stricken with sadness.
Molecules dance with a delicate madness.
Below, fireflies flicker with delight;
together they mingle, excitement in flight.

Deep in the cotton, the droplets form,
gathering in millions and brewing a storm.
Sheltered now by the forest canopy high,
the insects heed the warning of the night sky.

Swiftly they exit their ethereal nest,
winds fiercely swirling, blowing in from the
West.
It's late now, the fireflies call it a night;
they tuck in their wings and outen the light.

The descent towards the Earth, freeing and calm,
slipping through humid air - a peaceful balm.
Silently, the world is comfortably at rest;
tomorrow's a new day and courageous quest.

Into a current, the droplet seamlessly blends,
traveling down an embankment and then a sharp
bend.

The excitement so fierce, he could practically scream,
life for these atoms, returning home to a stream.

Mourning Stardust

Heavy is the heart, cursed by defeat;
a substantial sadness is leaving me weak.
An elusive opportunity just out of reach,
a dream left behind upon the shores of a beach.

They say every failure is a lesson to learn,
a chance to ignite, a fortune to burn.
How does one progress after an opportunity slips
through our fingers like sand from such tight
grips?

Heavy is my heart as it carries the light,
as a beacon of strength through the darkest
night.
Longing will forever linger, yet so does the trust
in the magic of creation—breathing life into
stardust.

Today's Sun

I saw the sunrise this morning,
flying by at 65 miles per hour.
The hustle and bustle of a nine to five.

The canvas of the sky,
a beautiful installation piece,
bathed in pinks,
dampened by the sapphire clouds.
The orange glow of the sun's rays
envelopes the corner of the page.

Moisture in the atmosphere,
dances on the horizon dressed in ombre pastels.
It's in this metal box on wheels,
where I see the best part of today's sun.

Cosmic Confidence in Haiku

The sun never thinks,
am I qualified for this?
Show up and shine bright

The moon never feels
wavering significance
through all its phases

We must move through life
be present and connected
on our soul's journey

Fearlessly advance
take a risk and learn from it
move confidently

Embrace the sunlight
dance underneath the moonlight
cosmic connection

Emotional Feast

Trigger warning: this poem is about binge eating
disorder.

The year of tears I never shed,
I processed them with food instead.
Fistfuls of fruit snacks and gummy bears,
Indulging in my many food affairs.

Cookies, pastries, cinnamon buns,
The dopamine hit is oh so fun.
I must go on until it's done,
Tomorrow I'll quit this addiction.

Consuming my every thought,
My hyperfixation has my stomach in knots.
It doesn't matter, I power through,
Ice cream, chocolate, and macaroons too.

I might as well just finish it now,
I chose to eat just like a cow.
Bury the wrappers deep in the trash,
The evidence of my binge now gone in a flash.

My disordered eating,
Is my attempt to avoid feeling,
Following the year of tears I never shed.

Together, with Love

I fondly recall the night we first met,
many years fall between but I'll never forget,
It started with a table for two, then seats at the bar,
ending the night with a kiss by my car.

Conversation flowed like a perfect pour,
this felt like the universe had opened the door.
After years of hiding from who I really was,
my attraction to her was giving me a buzz.

My heart refreshed and brand new
that night's revelation, a destiny anew.
From then on, clear and bright,
my life was quickly taking flight.

Renting a U-Haul, as typical lesbian do,
our future together now gaily in view.
United, we conquered feats once deemed unlikely,
grateful for this bond we hold so tightly.

To Vegas we flew, as two lovebirds do,
we got married, celebrated, and gambled too.
I was elated to be at the altar with you,

adorned in something old, new, borrowed, and
blue.

Through buying a home and fertility stuff,
the things we endured felt so tough,
But as I look at our lives these days,
I will always find solace in your embrace.

An Unexpected Visit

I'd like to think you knew I was there,
it'd been years since I stopped to visit and share.
You see, I didn't expect to find myself here,
but thanks to some errands that brought me near.

The weather was beautiful, bright, and sunny,
flashbacks of memories tinted in honey,
flooded my brain, bringing a tear to my eye,
it's been years since we shared our forever
goodbye.

I crouched down close and and started to cry,
"I miss you dearly," I shouted to the sky.
Every day I wish that you were still here
I hold our memories so close and near.

It's been seven years since your passing,
in my heart your legacy lives on, everlasting.
So much has happened during that time,
we have a son now, energetic and kind.

I wish so badly that you could meet him,
he has your heart, smile, and even your chin.
I believe it was you who helped send him our
way,
I long for you to be here, I've so much more to
say.

Unexpected Brothers

Sometimes I hear you in the early morning hours
Questioning life and why humans take showers
Under the window seems like your favorite
place to nap
I like it the most when you lay on my lap
Nighttime is when we cuddle in bed
Together we sleep head to head
Squints, you're the best cat I've ever had

Belly rubs and homemade treats
Ready to snuggle, your hair sprinkles the sheet
Always happy to see us with a stuffy in tow
Daily you make our smiles grow
Yellow lab Brady, you fill us with love

An Ode to Pocket Books

At the corner of Wheatland Ave, it stands,
a Victorian gem, with ornate bands.
Its yellow façade adorned in delicate grace,
a timeless beauty in a modern space.

Amidst the hustle of the city's beat,
this bookstore is more than a tranquil retreat.
A place to linger, to browse, to roam,
to find a piece of oneself, that feels like home.

The comforting scent of printed prose fills the
air,
a cozy nook alongside a velvety pink chair,
all the magic found within these walls,
where imaginations soar and sadness falls.

"Hello and welcome" floats proudly from the
right,
the warm greeting soft, a calming delight.
Floor-length bookshelves blanket every wall,
the spines of novels decorate a harlequin sprawl.

Friends come and gather to chat and discuss,
book club begins, voices hushed.
In this sanctuary, minds align,

under the chandelier's gentle glow, stories
entwine.

On Wheatland Ave, this bookstore stands tall,
a beacon of light for readers big and small.
a corner of solace in a bustling scene,
where journeys begin forever serene.

Support Pocket Books - the eclectic feminist
bookstore that calls Lancaster, Pennsylvania
home at https://www.pocketbooksshop.com/

My Mama Era

Smudgy fingers stain the glass door,
cars and crayons litter the floor,
Legos ®, markers, and children's board games—
the visual clutter ices the blood in my veins.

Why am I like this? Can't I let it be?
One day this clutter of toys I'll no longer see.
I'll be wishing to have this time back,
so for now I will cherish every time I open his
snack.

The evolution of his life, unfolding right in front
of me—
Why does time feel like it's trying to flee?
There's a bittersweetness to it all,
in watching our children grow up and stand tall.

I need to take a step back,
and keep my feelings in check.
Hidden in the chaos lies beauty too,
in the laughter, mess, and bonding with you.

Frisson Feelings

Fireworks beneath the flesh
Rise and fall from the core
Inside the electricity flows
Sensational sounds, euphoria
Scratching that itch deep within the brain
Outward flowing - goosebumps ripple
Nexus between music and mood

Haiku Ritual

Collect the supplies
Candles, crystals, paper, pen,
Set the space. Begin

Setting intentions
Write it into existence
Manifest your life

Draw from the cards and
Look to the stars for guidance
Direction, resolve

Reflect, grow, expand
Elevate your vibration
Adored universe

A Gift for my Beloved

A bundle of dried flowers,
baby's-breath entwined with lavender's sweet
hue
pampas grass, and dried plumes—
the finishing touches include
three tiny flowers of pink, yellow, and blue.

A stunning arrangement bound by twine,
wrapped in decorative tissue paper,
that resembles a page from the Times—
a gift for my beloved.

Scars Unraveled

Trigger warning: this poem is about
dermatillomania.

Fingernail tracing paths unseen,
unraveling edges where scars convene,
Flesh and mind collide in silent prayer,
a battle waged alone in the depths of despair.

Casually canvassing the calluses,
searching for snags on the surface of skin,
Cuticles, hang nails, and paper cuts,
the mind meticulously taking notes.

Pick the skin until it bleeds,
peel it back, exposing what's beneath,
The pain offering blissful peace,
emotions gone, thoughts release.

Delicate hands now tender and raw,
stained red - an unsightly scar,
Yet amidst the pain, resilience found,
in healing touch, new strength is bound.

My Jetta's Journey

It was in July of 2013,
my sights set on a car, shiny and clean.
I saved for months to finally buy
a Volkswagen Jetta I could practically cry.

The sleek body so moody- a midnight blue,
sights of the open road now coming to view.
I signed the papers and bought my first car,
I was ready to travel near and far.

Across the years, through miles we'd roam,
behind the wheel truly felt like home.
I think of all the memories made,
the love I have for this car will never fade.

My loyal sidekick it weathered every storm,
kept me safe, comfortable, and warm.
From beach trips to my son's first day at
daycare,
Its legacy it'll leave is beyond compare.

As I write this now ten and a half years later,
my car is ready to meet its creator.
My '09 Jetta is falling apart,
as its engine falters and troubles start.

As I bid farewell to my faithful companion,
recollections flood my mind like a vast canyon.
Through highs and lows, it stood by my side,
a source of comfort, on life's wild ride.

Winter Reflection: A Series of Haiku

The sugary scent
Winter season is aglow
Nature's silent show

Overwhelming peace
Confetti swirls of snowfall
Velvety and white

Crisp, crunchy, crackle
The fresh snowfall, sheen and white
Bundle up and play

A Portrait of Wonder

All around wonders unfold,
there lives a child, four and a half years old.
With creativity wild and imagination free,
he sketches his dreams for all to see.

It's during playtime he finds delight,
building houses for toys, tall and bright.
With every piece, his newest creation,
forever fueling his endless innovation.

On hikes through forests, he loves to explore,
each leaf and twig, he'll stop to adore.
Quickly his little feet run with glee,
natural curiosity exciting and free.

To the rhythm of the wind's soft sigh,
he'll dance beneath the painted cerulean sky.
His contagious giggle, a joyful sound,
can be heard high above the busy playground.

Reading books, snuggled up tight,
every page a welcomed sight.
Tuck him in, all ready for sleep,
soon he'll be off counting the sheep.

A child of wonder, pure and bright,
in his world, everything's just right.
I hope his imagination's spark won't wane,
may creativity forever reign.

The Carousel's Loop

Upon the carousel we go round and round,
the painted horses colorful and profound.
The first horse an energetic, vibrant hue,
adorned with flowers, a life anew.

Years pass by as time goes on
adolescence life has come and gone.
The second horse bears a shade of cobalt,
the visual sadness of emotions unfought.

As it spins, the colors rearrange,
the carousel of life in a constant swirl of change.
The next horse appears in deep cherry red,
the engagement ring reflecting light ahead.

Yet still we ride and hope remains,
the memory of life's beauty sustains.
The somber horse of solemn grey,
enhances the darkness in our way.

Each painted horse, a tale untold,
the cycle of life will always unfold.
Atop a golden horse of glory days,
one enjoys the sunshine through the haze.

More time has come to pass,
tarnished now the accents of brass.
Soon enough the colors fade,
during the calliaphone's parting serenade.

Dinner at Mama's Pizza

Mama's Pizza Shop
The perfect dinner backdrop
A new tradition

A mommy and son
Catching up and having fun
Pizza dinner date

Thick pizza crust smiles
Sharing stories from the week
Eating together

Two saucy slices
Spotted with pepperoni
Garlic, herbs, and spices

Mother Nature's Symphony

Sky scraping woodland, standing stoic and tall,
beside them, our significance feels diminished
and small.
Thousands of species claim this space their own;
when taking a hike, one's never truly alone.

The canopy above, tickled by wind's whispers;
below, sunlight and shade dances and flickers.
Leaves clap together in a round of applause;
Mother Nature is the ultimate boss.

Roots clutch the soil in a tight fist;
their intricate systems below turn and twist.
Moss-covered stones and fallen logs tell tales
of ancient times and forgotten trails.

Thick in the brush of ferns and wildflowers,
animals and insects dance and play for hours.
Darting squirrels and birds, staccato songs,
blend to create nature's sing-along.

Dusk approaches as the forest whispers a
lullaby;
a delicate melody beneath the moonlit sky.

Crickets and grasshoppers tune their
instruments;
the sounds of this woodland so blissfully
intense.

And Thus

Superficial sex bathed in deep red hues
An astute intriguer disguised as a deer
Lavish life, desirable from an outsider's
perspective
Time does not exist here
Broken piano
Unhinged and manic feels quite the norm
Rich but not wealthy - intellectually speaking
Never let them know your next move

Dare I say that I've
Rewatched this film a million times
Every replay I find something new
A jarring dialogue about the elite
Metaphor, symbolism, camera angle
Scarlet scandal